Bond

Verbal Reasoning

Practice Activities

5–6 years

Frances Down

OXFORD

UNIVERSITY PRESS

OXFORD
UNIVERSITY PRESS

Great Clarendon Street, Oxford, OX2 6DP, United Kingdom

Oxford University Press is a department of the University of Oxford.
It furthers the University's objective of excellence in research, scholarship,
and education by publishing worldwide. Oxford is a registered trade mark of
Oxford University Press in the UK and in certain other countries

First published by Nelson Thornes Ltd in 2013

British Library Cataloguing in Publication Data
Data available

978-1-4085-1878-6

10 9 8 7 6 5 4 3

Printed in China

Acknowledgements

Page make-up: OKS Prepress, India

Although we have made every effort to trace and contact all
copyright holders before publication this has not been possible in all
cases. If notified, the publisher will rectify any errors or omissions at
the earliest opportunity.

Links to third party websites are provided by Oxford in good faith
and for information only. Oxford disclaims any responsibility for
the materials contained in any third party website referenced in
this work.

Introduction

What is Bond?

This book is part of the Bond range of assessment papers for verbal reasoning, which provides thorough and continuous practice of all the key verbal reasoning content from ages 5 to 12. Bond's verbal reasoning resources are ideal preparation for many different kinds of tests and exams – from SATs to the 11+ and other secondary school selection exams.

What does this book cover?

Verbal reasoning questions can be grouped into five distinct categories: sorting words, selecting words, anagrams, coded sequences and logic. This book lays the earliest foundations through early practice of these different categories. One of the key features of the Bond range of assessment papers is that each one practises a wide variety of skills and question types so that children are always challenged to think.

The age given on the cover is for guidance only. As the papers are designed to be reasonably challenging for the year group, any one child may find him or herself working above or below the stated age. The important thing is that children are always encouraged by their performance. Working at the right level is the key to this.

What does the book contain?

- 20 papers – each paper contains 15 questions.
- Scoring devices – there are scoring boxes in the margins and a progress chart at the back of the book. Encouraging the child to colour in the chart as they go along and to try to beat their score can be very motivating.
- Answers – these are located in an easily removed central pull-out section.

How can you use this book?

One of the great strengths of the Bond range of assessment papers is their flexibility. They can be used at home, school and by tutors to:

- provide regular verbal reasoning practice in bite-sized chunks
- highlight strengths and weaknesses in the core skills
- identify individual needs
- set homework
- set timed practice tests – allow about 25 minutes.

Remember, more support, advice, information and free resources are available at www.bond11plus.co.uk.

1–4 Write these words in the correct groups.

red   sister   mother   blue

family	colours

4

Write these words in alphabetical order.

The alphabet has been written out to help you.

a b c d e f g h i j k l m n o p q r s t u v w x y z

Example van car bus _bus car van_

5 toy   baby   dog   _____

6 yell   talk   cry   _____

7 nose   hair   eye   _____

3

Add a letter to the front of the capital letters so that the sentences make sense.

8 I like to read a ____OOK.

9 Please close the ____OOR.

10 At night time, I go to ____LEEP.

11 It is so cold that it might ____NOW.

4

Work out the missing number.

12 6   7   8   ____

13 4   3   2   ____

14 11   12   13   ____

15 2   4   6   ____

4

Paper 2

Underline the word in each line that uses only the first six letters of the alphabet.

The first six letters of the alphabet have been written out to help you.

a b c d e f

Example   cat   bar   <u>bed</u>

1 fat   rag   fed

2 van   cab   car

3 bad   can   mat

Underline the two words, one from each group, that are closest in meaning.

Example   (<u>shut</u>, open)   (<u>close</u>, window)

4 (huge, sad)   (big, tiny)

5 (jolly, odd)   (strange, made)

6 (cold, small)   (well, little)

Underline the two words that are made from the same letters.

Example   <u>tea</u>   pot   <u>eat</u>

7 rat   rot   tar

8 pat   tap   lap

9 odd   dog   god

Take one letter from the word in capital letters to make a new word.

The meaning of the new word is given in the clue.

Example AUNT an insect <u>ant</u>

10 PALE a friend, a chum _____

11 TILE wear round your neck _____

12 KIND a baby goat or a child _____ ◯ 3

Underline one word from the brackets so that the sentences make sense.

Example The (car, <u>cow</u>) was eating grass.

13 Dad made a (cup, bag) of tea.

14 We stopped as the traffic light turned (white, red).

15 The little bird had five (eggs, stones) in her nest. ◯ 3

Paper 3

Sort the letters to make a proper word.

1 Sam hit the ball with a TAB _____.

2 I like AMJ _____ on my bread and butter.

3 Our OGD _____ barks at the postman.

Underline the odd one out in the group of words.

4 pig   cow   sheep   farm

5 grape   orange   carrot   apple

6 school   sock   shoe   shorts

Work out the missing letter.

The alphabet has been written out to help you.

A B C D E F G H I J K L M N O P Q R S T U V W X Y Z

7 E   F   G   ____

8 W   X   Y   ____

9 M   N   O   ____

3

3

3

Underline the word in the brackets closest in meaning to the word in capital letters.

Example UNHAPPY (unkind, <u>sad</u>)

10 HAPPY   (glad, sorry)

11 PALE   (dark, light)

12 NOISY   (loud, bark)

3

In a code, BEAD is written as 5 8 3 2.

    B E A D

    5 8 3 2

Work out these words using the same code.

13 5 3 2 _____

14 5 8 2 _____

15 5 8 8 _____

3

Paper 4

Underline the word in the brackets that is most opposite in meaning to the word in capital letters.

> **Example** WIDE (broad, <u>narrow</u>)

1 HOT   (cold, warm)

2 DOWN   (out, up)

3 THIN   (fit, fat)

4 QUICK   (slow, fast)

4

Underline the one word that **cannot be made** from the letters of the word in capital letters.

> **Example** STATE   tea   sat   <u>toe</u>   ate

5 GRAPE   rap   peg   gap   ram

6 WRITE   wet   rat   tie   wit

7 BREAD   bid   bad   red   are

8 TEARS   sat   rat   tea   sit

4

Change the first word of the third pair in the same way as the other pairs.

> **Example** dig, dog fig, fog big, _bog_

9 put, pit but, bit hut, _____

10 hog, hug bog, bug jog, _____

11 can, cane pan, pane man, _____

If a = 1, b = 2 and c = 3, work out the answers.

12 a + c = ____

13 b + c = ____

14 c − a = ____

15 b − a = ____

Paper 5

Underline the odd one out in the group of words.

Example   black   <u>king</u>   purple   green

1 duck   hen   swan   worm

2 leg   chair   sofa   stool

3 speak   run   chat   talk

4 four   six   ten   number

4

Underline one word from the brackets so that the sentences make sense.

Example   The (car, <u>cow</u>) was eating grass.

5 I am writing with my new (pen, cage).

6 Please brush your (wall, hair).

7 My cat likes to sit in a (muddy, sunny) spot.

8 Please sit (down, in).

4

Underline the two words, one from each group, that are the most opposite in meaning.

9 (rain, day)   (night, fall)

10 (ask, in)   (find, out)

11 (hard, busy)   (jump, easy)

12 (near, crying)   (far, sad)   4

Underline the one word that **cannot be made** from the letters of the word in capital letters.

13 CRANE   can   cat   ran   ear

14 PLEAT   eat   pat   pal   pit

15 SPIKE   pea   pie   ski   sip   3

Paper 6

Underline the word in the brackets closest in meaning to the word in capital letters.

> **Example** UNHAPPY (unkind, <u>sad</u>)

  1 CLOSE   (near, far)

  2 MAT   (floor, rug)

  3 BEGIN   (end, start)   **3**

Underline the word in each line that has two vowels.

The vowels have been written out to help you.

a   e   i   o   u

> **Example** chat <u>made</u> walk

  4 zips   nice   back

  5 gone   halt   then

  6 soft   belt   fire   **3**

Add a letter to the front of the capital letters so that the sentences make sense.

> **Example** Grass is <u>G</u>REEN.

  7 The ____AIN has made me wet.

  8 We had roast chicken for our ____UPPER.

  9 Tom writes with his ____EFT hand.   **3**

In a code, CART is written as ◊ ● □ ⌂.

C A R T
◊ ● □ ⌂

Work out these words using the same code.

10 ◊ ● □ _____

11 □ ● ⌂ _____

12 ◊ ● ⌂ _____

3

Work out the missing number.

Example 1 2 3 <u>4</u>

13 10   20   30   ____

14 7   6   5   ____

15 1   3   5   ____

3

Paper 7

Work out the missing letter.

The alphabet has been written out to help you.

A B C D E F G H I J K L M N O P Q R S T U V W X Y Z

Example   A   B   C   <u>D</u>

1   R   S   T   ____

2   F   E   D   ____

3   V   W   X   ____

4   V   U   T   ____

4

Write these words in alphabetical order.

The alphabet has been written out to help you.

a b c d e f g h i j k l m n o p q r s t u v w x y z

Example   van   car   bus   <u>bus   car   van</u>

5   tin   can   pot   _____

6   ill   mud   boy   _____

7   zip   net   ask   _____

3

8–12 Write these words in the correct groups.

bike   shirt   car   lorry   skirt

transport	clothes

5

Underline the word in the brackets that is most opposite in meaning to the word in capital letters.

Example WIDE   (broad, <u>narrow</u>)

13 HIGH   (swing, low)

14 WET   (rain, dry)

15 GOOD   (bad, climb)

3

Paper 8

Underline the two words, one from each group, that are closest in meaning.

> **Example** (<u>shut</u>, open) (<u>close</u>, window)

   I (short, far)   (tall, small)

   2 (safe, leave)   (go, bath)

   3 (under, kind)   (below, thin)   **3**

Take one letter from the word in capital letters to make a new word.

The meaning of the new word is given in the clue.

> **Example** AUNT an insect <u>ant</u>

   4 PINK   liquid in a pen   _____

   5 CARD   you travel in it   _____

   6 HOUR   belongs to us   _____   **3**

If $a = 3$, $b = 4$ and $c = 2$, work out the answers.

   7 $a + b =$ ____

   8 $c + a =$ ____

   9 $b - c =$ ____   **3**

Sort the letters to make a proper word.

10 We took the paper FOF _____ the parcel.

11 He threw the rubbish into the BNI _____.

12 The dog jumped TUO _____ of the car.

3

Change the first word of the third pair in the same way as the other pairs.

13 pat, hat   pit, hit   put, _____

14 fit, fat   bit, bat   sit, _____

15 fan, ban   fin, bin   fun, _____

3

Paper 9

Underline the word in each line that uses only the first six letters of the alphabet.

The first six letters of the alphabet have been written out to help you.

a b c d e f

Example cat bar <u>bed</u>

  1 egg   leg   fee

  2 bee   bet   beg

  3 let   not   ace

3

Underline the two words that are made from the same letters.

Example <u>tea</u> pot <u>eat</u>

  4 nit   tin   win

  5 net   nut   ten

  6 nor   won   now

3

Underline the two words, one from each group, that are the most opposite in meaning.

Example (<u>early</u>, wake) (<u>late</u>, stop)

  7 (give, win)   (over, take)

  8 (add, odd)   (even, number)

  9 (love, sour)   (hate, neat)

3

Underline the odd one out in the group of words.

10 river   path   canal   stream

11 path   track   lorry   lane

12 puppy   lamb   kitten   adult   **3**

Underline the word in the brackets closest in meaning to the word in capital letters.

13 RUSH   (hurry, crawl)

14 LOOK   (see, think)

15 CHILLY   (warm, cold)   **3**

Paper 10

Underline the two words, one from each group, that are closest in meaning.

1 (run, away)   (jog, park)

2 (clap, race)   (boil, dash)

3 (bright, tight)   (dear, shiny)

4 (cruel, nice)   (unkind, wet)

4

Sort the letters to make a proper word.

5 Two add TOW _____ equals four.

6 Dogs bark and cows go OMO _____.

7 In the park there is a fallen LGO _____.

8 My dad always says "I love OUY _____".

4

Paper 1

1–4 family: sister, mother
   colours: red, blue
5 baby   dog   toy
6 cry   talk   yell
7 eye   hair   nose
8 B
9 D
10 S
11 S
12 9
13 1
14 14
15 8

Paper 2

1 fed
2 cab
3 bad
4 huge   big
5 odd   strange
6 small   little
7 rat   tar
8 pat   tap
9 dog   god
10 pal
11 tie
12 kid
13 cup
14 red
15 eggs

Paper 3

1 bat
2 jam
3 dog
4 farm
5 carrot
6 school
7 H
8 Z
9 P
10 glad

11 light
12 loud
13 BAD
14 BED
15 BEE

Paper 4

1 cold
2 up
3 fat
4 slow
5 ram
6 rat
7 bid
8 sit
9 hit
10 jug
11 mane
12 4
13 5
14 2
15 1

Paper 5

1 worm
2 leg
3 run
4 number
5 pen
6 hair
7 sunny
8 down
9 day   night
10 in   out
11 hard   easy
12 near   far
13 cat
14 pit
15 pea

Paper 6

1 near
2 rug

3 start
4 nice
5 gone
6 fire
7 R
8 S
9 L
10 CAR
11 RAT
12 CAT
13 40
14 4
15 7

Paper 7

1 U
2 C
3 Y
4 S
5 can   pot   tin
6 boy   ill   mud
7 ask   net   zip
8–12 transport: bike, car, lorry
     clothes: shirt, skirt
13 low
14 dry
15 bad

Paper 8

1 short   small
2 leave   go
3 under   below
4 ink
5 car
6 our
7 7
8 5
9 2
10 off
11 bin
12 out
13 hut
14 sat
15 bun

Paper 9

1 fee
2 bee
3 ace
4 nit   tin
5 net   ten
6 won   now
7 give   take
8 odd   even
9 love   hate
10 path
11 lorry
12 adult
13 hurry
14 see
15 cold

Paper 10

1 run   jog
2 race   dash
3 bright   shiny
4 cruel   unkind
5 two
6 moo
7 log
8 you
9 10
10 11
11 9
12 20
13 book
14 bags
15 dog

Paper 11

1 come   go
2 thick   thin
3 strong   weak
4 cave   jump   play
5 best   king   very
6 clay   high   must
7–11 weather: rain, snow
     face: ear, nose, eye

A2

12 X
13 G
14 W
15 J

Paper 12

1 shout
2 old
3 full
4 sit
5 fan
6 son
7 P
8 R
9 W
10 hat
11 cat
12 rug
13 RAW
14 EAR
15 ARE

Paper 13

1 gate
2 goat
3 moon
4 pit   tip
5 saw   was
6 has   ash
7 present
8 speak
9 soak
10 TAR
11 ART
12 FAR
13 sea
14 tan
15 how

Paper 14

1 paper
2 month
3 lunch

4 paint
5 sea
6 the
7 leg
8 fur
9 3
10 4
11 1
12 coat
13 hole
14 vase
15 laces

Paper 15

1 win
2 last
3 hard
4 RAM
5 MAP
6 RAP
7–11 colours: purple, pink
     drinks: squash, water, juice
12 W
13 C
14 B
15 B

Paper 16

1 cat
2 rod
3 pat
4 why
5 pea   ape
6 pan   nap
7 gas   sag
8 bat
9 pip
10 bit
11 hot
12 rot
13 rat
14 in
15 ball

Paper 17

1 bone
2 school
3 cream
4 9
5 15
6 8
7 rain
8 coat
9 plane
10 CAT
11 COT
12 ACT
13 hug   cuddle
14 cry   sob
15 long   tall

Paper 18

1–5 seaside: sand, waves
      pets: rabbit, dog, cat
6 sun
7 and
8 sad
9 hot
10 sew
11 car
12 nut
13 OUR
14 ROT
15 OUT

Paper 19

1 hide   find
2 dirty   clean
3 under   over
4 pot
5 men
6 ill
7 fox   gun   hen
8 box   jam   top
9 hut   mop   wax
10 K
11 V
12 S
13 C
14 B
15 W

Paper 20

1 BUS
2 BUT
3 TUB
4 animal
5 bench
6 park
7 squirrel
8 rid
9 set
10 ill
11 wet
12 sky
13 six
14 bag
15 the

Work out the missing number.

9 7   8   9   _____

10 5   7   9   _____

11 12   11   10   _____

12 5   10   15   _____

4

Underline one word from the brackets so that the sentences make sense.

13 I am reading an exciting (meal, book).

14 We packed our (bags, hair) and went on holiday.

15 We walked our (cow, dog) in the park.

3

Paper 11

Underline the two words, one from each group, that are the most opposite in meaning.

Example (<u>early</u>, wake) (<u>late</u>, stop)

1 (come, in)   (arrive, go)

2 (think, thick)   (thin, fat)

3 (strong, new)   (weak, walk)

3

Write these words in alphabetical order.

The alphabet has been written out to help you.

a b c d e f g h i j k l m n o p q r s t u v w x y z

Example van   car   bus   <u>bus   car   van</u>

4 jump   play   cave   _____

5 very   king   best   _____

6 high   clay   must   _____

3

7–11 Write these words in the correct groups.

ear   nose   rain   snow   eye

weather	face

5

Work out the missing letter.

The alphabet has been written out to help you.

A B C D E F G H I J K L M N O P Q R S T U V W X Y Z

Example   A   B   C   _D_

12 U   V   W   _____

13 A   C   E   _____

14 Z   Y   X   _____

15 G   H   I   _____

4

Paper 12

Underline the word in the brackets that is most opposite in meaning to the word in capital letters.

> **Example**   WIDE   (broad, <u>narrow</u>)

1 WHISPER   (count, shout)

2 YOUNG   (new, old)

3 EMPTY   (full, even)   **3**

Change the first word of the third pair in the same way as the other pairs.

> **Example**   dig, dog   fig, fog   big, <u>bog</u>

4 let, lit   bet, bit   set, _____

5 car, far   cat, fat   can, _____

6 win, won   tin, ton   sin, _____   **3**

Add a letter to the front of the capital letters so that the sentences make sense.

> **Example**   Grass is <u>G</u>REEN.

7 It was time to ____LAY in the park.

8 We take care crossing the busy ____OAD.

9 Meg's cat is ginger and ____HITE.   **3**

Take one letter from the word in capital letters to make a new word.

The meaning of the new word is given in the clue.

> **Example**   AUNT   an insect   <u>ant</u>

10 THAT   a cap   _____

11 COAT   an animal   _____

12 RUNG   a mat   _____   3

In a code, WEAR is written as 3 5 7 2.

   W E A R
   3 5 7 2

Work out these words using the same code.

13 2 7 3   _____

14 5 7 2   _____

15 7 2 5   _____   3

Paper 13

Underline the word in each line that has two vowels.

The vowels have been written out to help you.

a   e   i   o   u

Example   chat   <u>made</u>   walk

1 wand   help   gate

2 goat   calf   lamb

3 star   moon   dark   **3**

Underline the two words that are made from the same letters.

Example   <u>tea</u>   pot   <u>eat</u>

4 pit   pod   tip

5 saw   was   see

6 had   has   ash   **3**

Underline the word in the brackets closest in meaning to the word in capital letters.

Example   UNHAPPY   (unkind, <u>sad</u>)

7 GIFT   (live, present)

8 SAY   (speak, with)

9 WET   (soak, warm)   **3**

In a code, RAFT is written as 3 4 5 6.

R A F T
3 4 5 6

Work out these words using the same code.

10 6 4 3 _____

11 4 3 6 _____

12 5 4 3 _____ 3

Underline the one word that **cannot be made** from the letters of the word in capital letters.

| Example | STATE | tea | sat | toe | ate |

13 BEAT   bet   bat   sea   eat

14 THEN   tan   net   the   hen

15 BOWL   low   owl   bow   how   3

Paper 14

Underline the odd one out in the group of words.

1 square   circle   paper   triangle

2 May   June   July   month

3 lunch   knife   fork   spoon

4 yellow   paint   blue   white

4

Sort the letters to make a proper word.

5 We went for a swim in the ASE _____.

6 Someone is knocking at HET _____ door.

7 I fell and cut my GEL _____.

8 My cat has lovely soft URF _____.

4

If a = 3, b = 4 and c = 1, work out the answers.

9 b – c = ____

10 a + c = ____

11 b – a = ____

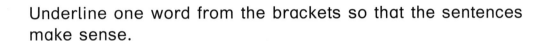

3

Underline one word from the brackets so that the sentences make sense.

Example   The (car, <u>cow</u>) was eating grass.

12 He did up the buttons on his (head, coat).

13 The rabbit ran down its (hole, back).

14 A (plate, vase) of flowers was on the table.

15 He did up the (laces, tie) on his shoes.

4

Paper 15

Underline the word in the brackets that is most opposite in meaning to the word in capital letters.

> **Example**   WIDE   (broad, <u>narrow</u>)

   1   LOSE   (lift, win)

   2   FIRST   (late, last)

   3   SOFT   (gentle, hard)   **3**

In a code, RAMP is written as $+ \times \div -$.

    R   A   M   P
    $+ \times \div -$

Work out these words using the same code.

   4   $+ \times \div$ _____

   5   $\div \times -$ _____

   6   $+ \times -$ _____   **3**

7–11 Write these words in the correct groups.

purple   squash   water   pink   juice

colours	drinks

5

Add a letter to the front of the capital letters so that the sentences make sense.

Example   Grass is GREEN.

12 We took our dog for a _____ALK up the hill.

13 She has five candles on her birthday _____AKE.

14 Zebras are _____LACK and white.

15 I like to ride my _____IKE.

4

Paper 16

Underline the one word that **cannot be made** from the letters of the word in capital letters.

> **Example**   STATE   tea   sat   <u>toe</u>   ate

1 CAGES   age   cat   gas   ace

2 BRAND   rod   and   ran   bad

3 TRAIN   nit   ran   tin   pat

4 WHITE   the   why   hit   wet   `4`

Underline the two words that are made from the same letters.

> **Example**   <u>tea</u>   pot   <u>eat</u>

5 pea   ape   pet

6 ban   pan   nap

7 gas   sag   gap   `3`

Take one letter from the word in capital letters to make a new word.

The meaning of the new word is given in the clue.

> **Example** AUNT   an insect   <u>ant</u>

   8 BATH   hit a ball with this   _____

   9 PIPE   an apple's seed   _____

 10 BITE   a little piece   _____

 11 SHOT   not cold   _____   ( ) 4

Change the first word of the third pair in the same way as the other pairs.

> **Example** dig, dog   fig, fog   big, <u>bog</u>

 12 hoot, hot   loot, lot   root, _____

 13 cut, cat   but, bat   rut, _____

 14 won, on   wan, an   win, _____

 15 fill, fall   hill, hall   bill, _____   ( ) 4

Paper 17

Underline one word from the brackets so that the sentences make sense.

> **Example** The (car, <u>cow</u>) was eating grass.

   1 The dog chewed on his (bone, fish).

   2 It is time for the end of (house, school).

   3 I like ice (cream, plate).

Work out the missing number.

> **Example** I 2 3 <u>4</u>

   4 3   5   7   _____

   5 12   13   14   _____

   6 11   10   9   _____

Underline the odd one out in the group of words.

> **Example** black <u>king</u> purple green

   7 winter   spring   rain   summer

   8 moon   star   sun   coat

   9 boat   canoe   ship   plane

In a code, COAT is written as Δ O ◊ ●.

C O A T
Δ O ◊ ●

Work out these words using the same code.

10 Δ ◊ ● _____

11 Δ O ● _____

12 ◊ Δ ● _____

3

Underline the two words, one from each group, that are closest in meaning.

13 (hug, bug)   (cuddle, bed)

14 (cry, laugh)   (talk, sob)

15 (break, long)   (tall, short)

3

Paper 18

1–5 Write these words in the correct groups.

rabbit   dog   sand   waves   cat

seaside	pets

5

Sort the letters to make a proper word.

Example   My mum drinks a cup of ETA _tea_.

6 The NUS _____ is shining brightly today.

7 All the boys NDA _____ girls go out to play.

8 When my friend left, I was DAS _____.

9 This fire is too TOH _____!

4

Underline the one word that **cannot be made** from the letters of the word in capital letters.

> **Example** STATE   tea   sat   <u>toe</u>   ate

10 HOUSE   she   use   hoe   sew

11 CHATS   has   sat   car   cat

12 TWINS   win   nut   wit   tin   ( ) 3

In a code, TOUR is written as c d e f.

    T O U R
    c d e f

Work out these words using the same code.

13 d e f   _____

14 f d c   _____

15 d e c   _____   ( ) 3

Paper 19

Underline the two words, one from each group, that are the most opposite in meaning.

1 (hide, look)   (see, find)

2 (hurry, dirty)   (clean, on)

3 (under, by)   (over, high)

⬤ 3

Take one letter from the word in capital letters to make a new word.

The meaning of the new word is given in the clue.

4 SPOT   a tub   _____

5 MEAN   grown-up boys   _____

6 FILL   unwell   _____

⬤ 3

Write these words in alphabetical order.

The alphabet has been written out to help you.

a b c d e f g h i j k l m n o p q r s t u v w x y z

7 gun   fox   hen   _____

8 jam   box   top   _____

9 wax   hut   mop   _____

⬤ 3

40

Work out the missing letter.

The alphabet has been written out to help you.

A B C D E F G H I J K L M N O P Q R S T U V W X Y Z

Example   A   B   C   <u>D</u>

10   H   I   J   ____

11   Y   X   W   ____

12   P   Q   R   ____

3

Add a letter to the front of the capital letters so that the sentences make sense.

Example   Grass is <u>G</u>REEN.

13   He ate his fish and ____HIPS.

14   I pushed my ____ABY brother in his pram.

15   I was tired so I ____ENT to bed.

3

Paper 20

In a code, BUST is written as ∨ ∧ > <.

B U S T
∨ ∧ > <

Work out these words using the same code.

1 ∨ ∧ >   _____

2 ∨ ∧ <   _____

3 < ∧ ∨   _____

3

Underline the odd one out in the group of words.

Example   black   <u>king</u>   purple   green

4 animal   lion   wolf   bear

5 boy   girl   bench   man

6 wall   roof   park   door

7 branch   leaves   trunk   squirrel

4

Underline the one word that **cannot be made** from the letters of the word in capital letters.

> **Example** STATE tea sat <u>toe</u> ate

8 DREAM   mad   arm   ear   rid

9 STAIR   air   set   rat   sit

10 BLINK   ink   bin   nib   ill

11 WHOSE   who   sew   wet   she   (4)

Sort the letters to make a proper word.

> **Example** My mum drinks a cup of ETA <u>tea</u>.

12 The birds are flying high in the YSK _____.

13 She is IXS _____ years old today.

14 May dropped her GAB _____ on the floor.

15 He climbed up TEH _____ stairs.   (4)